I AM STRONG, SMART & KIND

The back page of each illustration is blank to prevent ink bleed

TODAY SHAPES TOMORROW

Have you thought about the
kind of person you want to
be when you grow up?
Did you know that your thoughts
and beliefs today shape the
woman you will become tomorrow.
So let's focus on all that's great
about you and head towards
a shining bright future!

I AM CARING

I AM UNIQUE

I AM ME!

ONE FOR THE BOYS!
AVAILABLE NOW ON AMAZON

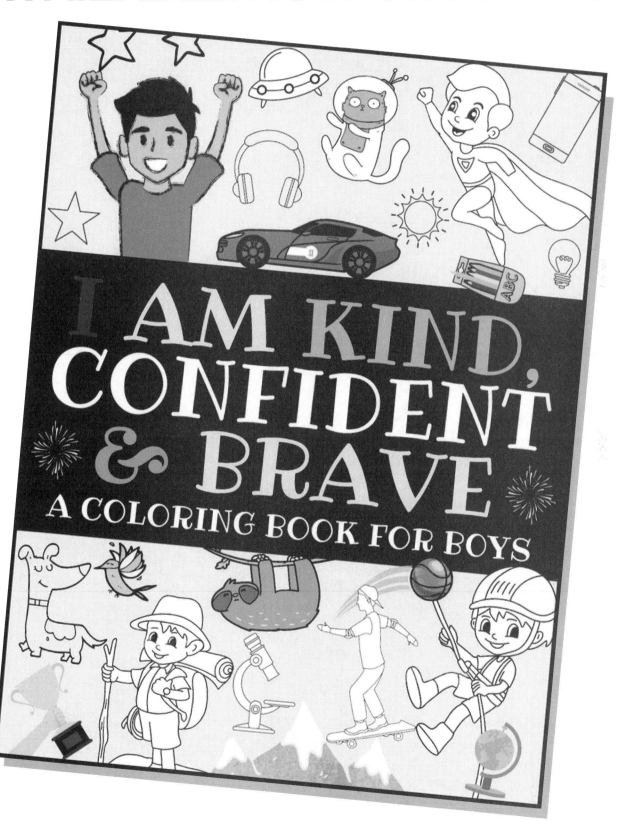

INSPIRATIONAL COLORING BOOK

OUR GIFT TO YOU!

Because you've done such a great job and looked at what it means to be strong, smart, creative, patient, thankful and all the other positive qualities, you can do it all again!

Here's every page once more. From us to you. Enjoy!

I AM CONFIDENT

I AM CREATIVE

I AM FAIR

I AM CURIOUS